MW00450741

To
Dad

Merry Xmas '87

Julie

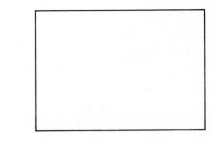

China Unknown

China Unknown

Introduction by David Bonavia

BOOKS

2 Two Hani women await their turn before marching in a great procession at the Water Splashing Festival, an annual event that many Chinese minority groups share with their counterparts in Southeast Asia. The Hani live in Yunnan Province along China's border with Burma, Laos and Vietnam.

5 In southern China's Guangdong Province, the people are remarkably creative in their choice and consumption of food. Nearly everything gets eaten: cats and dogs, wasp larvae, snakes, rats, ox penis, ants, monkeys, sea lice, civets and pangolins. "In the heavens, all that can fly are eaten except aeroplanes. On land, all with four legs are eaten except tables."

In a market, this owl awaits a buyer. After purchase it will be plucked, drawn, and boiled for soup. All around are the squeals, shrieks and yelps of various animals waiting for a similar end. In most cases the broth they produce is held to have aphrodisiac, medicinal as well as invigorating properties.

8 Unrestrained celebration marks the Chinese New Year in a rural Yunnanese village. On this day many families will eat day-long meals of up to sixty courses. "Eat, eat! Eat until you're dizzy." In previous years, from 1966 to 1978, such feasting and clamorous invitations to indulge would have been banned by a grim, prudish government. Now the traditional New Year rituals have reappeared, like the noisy and colourful lion dance, with its attendant jolly folk characters in large, pink head masks, symbols of prosperity. The mirrored ball in the right foreground represents a pearl that leads the procession, chased by lions and dragons.

Library of Congress catalogue card number 84-40121
Book code 84-01713

ISBN 0-8129-1141-5

Copyright © 1985 by China Guides Series Ltd. First printed 1985. All rights reserved. No part of this publication may be reproduced or transmitted in any form or by any means, electronic or mechanical, including photocopy, recording, or any information storage and retrieval system, without permission in writing from the publisher. Printed in Hong Kong for Times Books, 130 Fifth Avenue New York, New York 10011 by Mandarin Offset International, Ltd., Hong Kong.

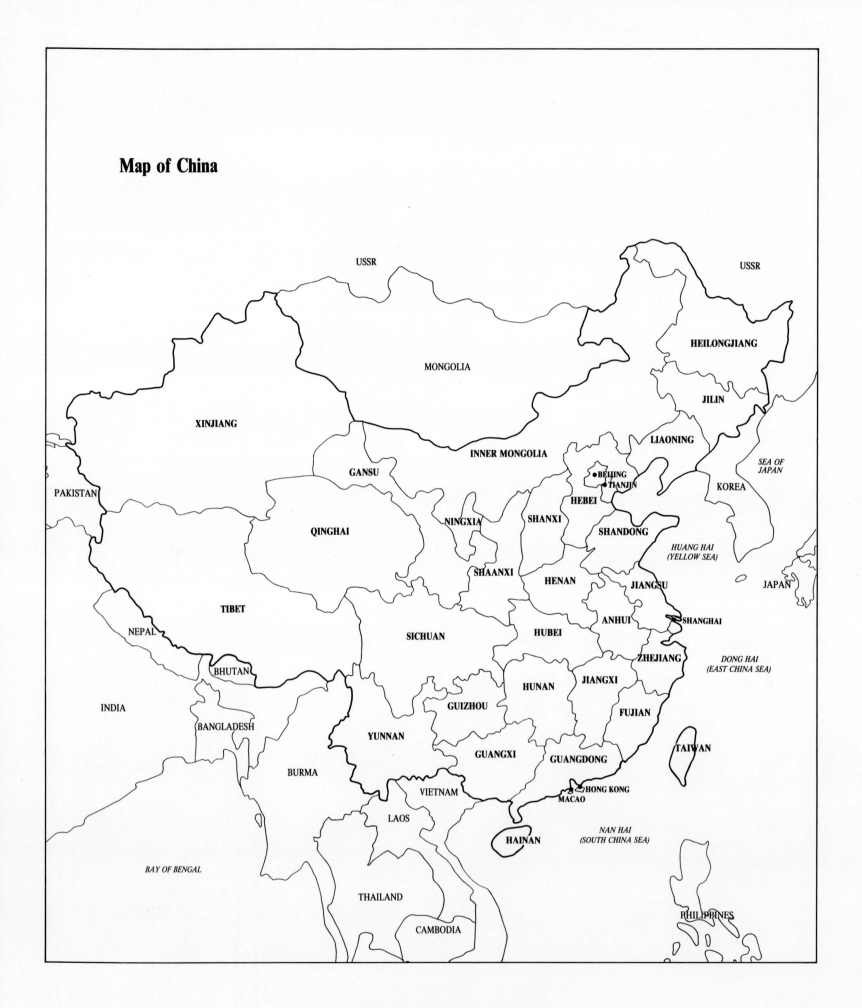

Map of China

Acknowledgements

The title of this book was not chosen without long deliberation and though some of the images may be familiar, I am confident that most of the material will be new to the reader. Many sources and individuals contributed to the contents but we would like to thank particularly two photographers whose work regularly appears in the National Geographic Magazine. Tom Nebbia and photo-journalist Wong How-Man set a standard which made assembling the book rewarding, exhilarating and a difficult act to follow.

Also to all the other photographers listed on the right without whose help and enthusiasm the book could not have taken this form; to designer Joan Law and editorial maestro Paddy Booz, our P.A. Yvonne Lam, colour separator Koji Sakai and his assistant Stephan Ng; to Norman de Brackinghe of Mandarin Offset, Robert Ducas, Louise Chinn, Chuck Stolbach, Margarita Bartlett, Judy Bonavia and May Holdsworth who all helped when the going got tough: Thank you.

Magnus Bartlett
China Guides
Hong Kong December 1984

Tom Nebbia
*2 5 10 18 25 31 38-39 75
77 82-83 85 118 131*

Wong How-Man
*12-13 16-17 36 42 43 46
52 57 62-63 65 66 72-73
76 78 80-81 137*

Paul Lau (Stock House)
*28 33 37 48 50-51 54 97
98 99 106 107 108 109
110 111 112 113 114-115
116-117 120-121 124-125
128 132 140-141 142*

Jacky Yip
*35 47 55 67 68 69 88-89
130*

Paddy Booz
8 61 74 84 86 87

Chan Yuen Kai/China Guides
*9 44 56 64 91 96 102
104 105*

*Wong How-Man Expedition/
Chan Yuen Kai*
40-41 45 49 53 58-59 60 79

George Chan
20 70 71 92-93 100-101 136

China Guides
3 11 92-93 129 133

William Ng (Stock House)
9 90 134-135 138-139

Leong Ka-Tai
26 103

Joan Law
119 126-127

Lew Roberts
122-123

Andreas Dannenberg
94-95

Contents

Introduction

The Seated Goat

The fierce attachment of most Chinese people to their homeland — even among those who have chosen to live abroad — is based partly on the poetry of the country's landscape, and partly on the unique life-style the land and climate have produced in each of its localities.

"These rivers and mountains, lovely as embroidery and brocade" — this is a favourite Chinese phrase to describe the astonishing variety of landscape, cultivated or barren, which is every Chinese person's right by birth.

Tilting Pacific-wards from the huge deserts and mountains of Central Asia and Tibet, the land draws its life and poetry from several great rivers, which alternately feed and destitute the people of the plains.

The Yangtze (in modern parlance the Chang Jiang or Long River) is taken as roughly dividing the country into north and south. The north is the heartland of China's ancient history, inhabited for at least half-a-million years by humanoid creatures. The south later became a centre or rather many centres of culture and the arts, greatly enriching the northern tradition, and engaging in commerce with overseas lands.

After nearly a millennium of bitter wars among the feudal states into which the land was divided, the south was brought under the control of emperors reigning in cities on the middle reaches of the Huang He, the Yellow River, some two centuries before the birth of Christ. Since then, with relatively brief interruptions, north and south have been a political if not entirely a cultural unity.

10 A painter puts the final touches to the face of Chairman Mao Zedong. These large portraits, increasingly rare, can still be seen in various parts of China. Since the fall of the notorious Gang of Four in 1976, most portraits of Mao, which used to adorn public places, have come down, and the personality cult built round him is being dismantled. This trend is reinforced by Vice Premier Deng Xiaoping's own refusal to be deified. State-supported artists, such as this young man, can make a living by painting billboards, advertisements, traffic signs, movie announcements and, occasionally, portraits.

Within this unity, enormous differences of life-style have evolved — and the photographs in this book help to show just how enormous they are. The borderlands are partly inhabited by ethnic minorities — Mongols, Tibetans, Uighurs, Miaos and more than fifty others. Some of these people have very ancient kinship ties with the Han or ethnic Chinese, as can be verified by studying their languages — though the ways of life of say, a Tibetan, a Miao and a Han are about as different from each other as one could conceive. With the fresh encouragement now being given to the minorities to keep up their old customs and wear traditional dress as well as speaking and writing their native languages (but also learning Chinese), they provide a large part of the fascination of modern China, even if they are massively outnumbered by the Han (approximately 65 million minority population to 1.1 billion Han).

Imagine the map of China as the outline of a seated goat. Northeast China (Manchuria) makes up the head, while Korea — of course not part of China — is the beard. The eastern and southern provinces of Jiangsu, Zhejiang, Guangdong and Guangxi make

up the breast and folded front legs. Yunnan and Tibet are the hind-legs and the rump, Xinjiang is the fat tail, and Inner Mongolia is the back and neck. Fanciful? Perhaps. But this simple mnemonic is an easy way of fixing in one's mind locations in China which at first seem to be nothing more than a jumble of hard-to-pronounce names.

The life and customs of the people are determined by climate and the land. Around Peking — which was originally built centuries before Christ as a frontier garrison town, not as the capital of China — raggedly dressed peasants scratch wheat, maize, and sorghum out of the tired earth, surviving only because they know well how to revive it year by year with natural fertilisers. Trees are sparse despite a big planting programme. Houses are built as south-facing courtyards to trap the sun in winter, and heating is from old anthracite stoves or just corn-stalks. Farther to the northeast — where China's frontiers march with those of Far Eastern Russia — the crops are coarser because the climate is tougher, and sheep, almost unknown in central and southern China, can flourish. Horses and deer are bred, mink is farmed.

Travelling down the east coast, one finds the character of the land and the people changing. The northerners are dour, fatalistic people who nevertheless have their own brand of humour to fall back on. As in most countries, the farther south you go, the more fun-loving and lively the people become.

In the eastern provinces south of Shandong, the people seem to glide effortlessly among the rice fields as they stand in their wooden or (nowadays) concrete-hulled boats — fishing, maintaining irrigation ditches, and herding ducks. Lush crops of rice reflect a brilliant, rich green light. The favourite foods are "fish and rice" which in Chinese carries almost the same connotation as "milk and honey."

Dominating the eastern region is the huge city of Shanghai, where the atmosphere is half-sinister, half-nostalgic. The ghosts of Japanese spies, British bankers, French missionaries and warlord generals still hang around the massive stone palaces to Mammon which the Europeans built to guard this cornerstone of their commerce in China from the mid-nineteenth till the mid-twentieth century.

Southward down the coast, rounding the "goat's knees", are the renowned tea plantations of Zhejiang — famous also for its silks — and the narrow strip of fertile soil backed by precipitous mountains which is Fujian Province. Hardwood and wood for pulp are lugged down from the mountains for export, and all along the coast there are fishing villages which under the new Chinese economic reforms are growing prosperous off their catches of fish, prawns, crabs, lobsters and abalone, as well as the gathering of edible seafood popular in Japan. Old customs die hard in the villages of remote Fujian, which is hard to penetrate from China's interior, and lavish peasant festivals for marriages and funerals are still common, despite the disapproval of the authorities.

To the south, Guangdong Province contains some of the richest farming country and fisheries, from where Chinese migrants have spread out all over the world in search of their fortune. Brash, mercenary Hong Kong — under British rule until 1997 — glitters and pulses with the energy of its modern manufacturing and commerce. Squat oil-rigs dot the South China Sea, drilling for the oil and gas forecast by geologists.

At the Vietnamese border — nowadays a troubled one — the Chinese coastline ends amidst the astonishing, near-vertical rock cliffs called karst, which cover Guangxi and especially the tourist beauty-spot of Guilin. From here inland lies some of China's loveliest landscape and its only truly temperate zone. In Yunnan Province, huge, blue, misty lakes set off the red-earthed terrace fields and emerald crops, the roads winding round the hills and mountains like coils of rope. This is the place where the biggest and most varied concentraton of ethnic minorities is found, with at least eight major groups each with its own

12, 13 Tug-of-war is one of many athletic and cultural events at the Langshan Festival, a yearly gathering of Tibetans in Gansu Province. Minority groups live throughout China although within each province they tend to be concentrated in a limited area. Gansu is a good example where nearly all Tibetans live within seven contiguous counties. Of China's one billion people sixty-five million belong to the so-called national minorities.

16, 17 On the upper Min River in western Sichuan, these loggers work with long bamboo poles to disentangle a pile of logs. The men are of the Qiang ethnic minority, brave and nimble; they do wear life-jackets but only light rice-straw sandals to protect their feet. The logs are floated all the way down the Min River to saw-mills near Chongqing. The Min is a major tributary of the Yangzi River.

distinctive and elaborate costumes, head adornments and delicately-wrought silver ornaments. Through mountainous Guizhou Province — still usually closed to foreigners — the land rises to the great plateau of Tibet, which resembles a huge altar-table abutting the Himalayas (and incidentally makes up the hind-legs of our "goat").

Tibet, despite nearly thirty-five years of Chinese rule, is still a land of ghosts and demons, spells, charms, sacrifices, bead-telling, prayer-wheels, self-prostrating believers, incense, and lamps endlessly fuelled with yak butter. In gloomy temples the walls are peopled with horrific images of souls and torturers in hell, as well as the serene Buddha statues which promise the believer relief, and Hindu gods practising esoteric sexual acts.

To the north, the "goat's hindquarters" are traced by the enormous Xinjiang region, where Uighurs, Kazakhs and other ancient Turkic people use centuries-old underground irrigation systems to grow lush grapes and cool, juicy water-melons. Around them stand ruined cities where Buddhist kingdoms flourished during Europe's Dark Ages. Public and religious festivals are numerous, and then everyone — man, woman and child — gets up to dance the sinuous arm-and-body movements of Central Asia, to music influenced by the Arabs, whose Islamic faith the indigenous people of Xinjiang have shared for centuries since the decline of Buddhism.

To the north, Uighurs and horse-riding Kazakhs rub shoulders with the Mongols, whose simple, semi-nomadic way of life, herding sheep and camels on horseback, is a far cry from the havoc they wrought when they came churning out of Asia in the Middle Ages to enslave Russia and batter at the gates of Vienna. They ruled China for over ninety years, and tried to invade Japan and Java. Tremendous horsemen though they were, they were no sailors, and were thrown back. The Vietnamese, too, under the two famous Truong Sisters, fought them to a standoff.

Within this fascinating loop of China's frontiers lies China proper — the Great Within, to borrow Maurice Collis' translation of the Chinese *danei*. There, hundreds of millions of people struggle to earn a living wage in the fields or in the steelworks, ordered around by all-too-often inept and unqualified officials. These people's schools, factories, clinics, universities and state farms are what the rulers of modern China want to show the outside world as proof of the progress they have made in their goal of quadrupling their country's national income by the year 2000.

One is tempted to wonder, who is better off? The Shanghai worker at his lathe eight hours a day, then queueing for vegetables and slumping into bed after an hour or two spent watching bad TV, or the Tibetan herdsman smoking his pipe and wrinkling his eyes at a fire of dried dung in a felt tent, wondering which godling to appease next day when the yak is going to calve?

Like Brocade and Embroidery

Western geologists have divided the territory of China into three great rocky masses of the pre-Cambrian period (before 570 million years BC). In accordance with their historic names, they are called Tibetia, Gobia and Cathaysia — Cathay being the mediaeval European word for China, probably derived by the Russians from the Khitans, a Tartar tribe on the Chinese borders.

Gobia (from the Mongol word for "desert") is a great, partly arid basin in Northwest China. Tibetia is an enormous plateau in the west and southwest, including parts of the country no longer incorporated in modern Tibet. From here great rivers irrigate Cathaysia — China proper — and large parts of Southeast Asia and India.

18 *In the deep countryside a small, isolated community has its own one-room schoolhouse. Although minority children are now generally taught in their own local languages, the greatest problem in education is the serious shortage of qualified teachers. This is due to rapid population growth, limited places at teacher training colleges, and the general disarray of education over the last twenty years. Even so there is a thirst for knowledge throughout China and families often make huge sacrifices to help a child's educational advancement.*

In ancient times, the Chinese called their two greatest rivers the He (Yellow River) and the Jiang (the Yangtze). Only later did these names become ordinary words meaning "river". The common feature of both rivers was their propensity to flood the plains in their middle and lower reaches, causing great devastation and loss of life, but also depositing silt and mud which improved the fertility of the land. The ancient Chinese chose as kings those who were most adept at river-control, particularly the building of earthen dykes.

The middle reaches of the banks of the He bear the first-known evidence of civilized man in China, from the second millennium BC, though traces of human settlement go back much further than that, and near Peking the remains of a stone-age man estimated at about 500,000 BC have been found.

By the end of the first millennium BC, the lands along and to the south of the Jiang were also settled by Hans (ethnic Chinese), to a large extent driving the distantly related indigenous people into the mountains of the west and southwest. By the time of the birth of Christ, the Chinese empire extended from Korea in the northeast to the Gansu Corridor in the northwest, the fringes of Tibet in the west, all the southern and eastern coastlines, and the northern coastal strip of Annam (Vietnam) in the south. Throughout these areas the Chinese cultivated rice, wheat and other grains, reared silkworms and wove silk — some of which was exported as far west as the Mediterranean — cast delicate bronzes (an art also developed by the smaller peoples in the southwest), wrote their language with a huge number of pictographic and ideographic characters, evolved political theories and carried on divination and religio-superstitious practices. They had the best equipped armies in the world with the exception of the Romans, and they had amassed an extensive knowledge of the natural world.

The shape of greater China — descending in steps from the Tibetan plateau, with smaller mountain ranges spaced in between as far as the coast — has brought about extensive run-off of rainwater, snowmelt and underground water generally in easterly and southerly directions, thus defining the agricultural possibilities of the heartland. Besides the Yellow River and the Yangtze there are extensive smaller river-systems in most parts of China proper, especially in the south.

At Lanzhou, in the semi-desert province of Gansu, the Yellow River comes leaping like a stallion through the hydroelectric plant that provides power for the chemical and steel industries which pollute the air worse than almost anywhere else in the country. Acid rain gnaws at the stonework of the museum where some of the best bronzes of Han times — including half-size models of ancient chariots — are kept in dimly lit rooms. Snaking down through the sand-dunes of Gansu, the river is joined by its big tributary, the Wei, on which stands the city of Xian (Changan) — capital of China under five different dynasties. Floods over the millennia have built up at least 3,000 feet of sand and silt on the North China Plain which the river traverses, through the fertile provinces of Henan and Shandong and into the Yellow Sea — the estuary having changed places several times.

The Yangtze, bearing less silt than its brother, nonetheless irrigates large areas of the rich province of Sichuan. It then squeezes into the series of gorges which drive it at immense speed and with terrific force down to the lowlands of Hubei, Jiangxi, Anhui and Jiangsu, entering the sea through a delta-shaped estuary north of Shanghai.

Historically, the Yangtze is regarded as dividing the two main areas of Chinese culture — the northern and the southern. Actually it would be more accurate to say the northwestern and the southeastern. Scholars regard northwest China as the home of the bureaucratic Confucian system of government which despised commerce and exalted agriculture — especially the cultivation of dry grains such as wheat and millet — and the heir to age-old fears of invasion by the horse-riding nomads of the north and west.

The south — Jiang Nan — is the home of the gentler and more luxurious culture which flowered especially from the Song Dynasty on (European early Middle Ages). It is the home of exotic foods and spices distrusted by the conservative northerners. It has cultivated contacts with the often warlike small tribes of the southwest, whilst often oppressing them beyond endurance. Its orientation is down the rivers and towards the East and South China Sea, gateways to the tropical lands of Southeast Asia with their rich Buddhist and Hindu cultures.

In the nineteenth century it was Jiang Nan that absorbed most quickly the new influences and ideas coming from Europe and America, so that revolutionary, anti-dynastic pressures arose there more rapidly than in the north, splitting the country in the early twentieth century.

Still today it is in the south — with access to Hong Kong and Portuguese-administered Macau — that the new influx of Western and Japanese capital and technology is transforming the face of China's backward industries.

"Like brocade and embroidery" — that is how the Chinese describe the infinite variety of landscape and natural beauty for which their country is famous. And that variety lies not just in the land, but in the people who inhabit it. Over half of China's land area has indigenous populations with wholly different styles of life and culture. Of these, the most fascinating are the Tibetans.

The Pastures in the Sky

Animal-herding nomads feel close to the heavens — the more so in China's high grasslands where centuries of religious thought has taught the unity of man, spirits and nature. The sky really does seem closer, perhaps because the clouds are as likely to be around or below you as above you.

To ascend a mountain anywhere else means to reach a summit and then think about going down by the same way as one came up, or by descending another slope. Approaching the places of the Tibetans, the alps of high Asia seem no more than huge and craggy foothills. The goal is not a summit but a gently singing plain of coarse grass. A huge inland lake laps its shore in the purest white crescents of foam: you feel you could almost reach out five miles and touch it. Landward are the heads and shoulders of more mountains, with more plateaux beyond their outlines; and the straight ribbon of a road going over the bumpy pasture's rim.

The grass is tough and slippery, scattered with tiny blue flowers round which dance still tinier mauve-and-blue butterflies. Enormous, shaggy black yaks stand around, the givers of rich milk and butter.

On the horizon some barley fields tell of the people's tastes in food. Dairy products, boiled mutton and barley meal are all a Tibetan needs the year round; sugar is a welcome luxury.

Race day! The long afternoon passes in a happy stupor of sun and sudden overcast. Every twenty minutes or so three riders scamper down the unmarked track with whoops and cries, the spectators joining in with shrill ululations. The winning rider swings his lariat in a whipping windmill round his head, and the race seems over before it has begun. The riders amble back casually without banter or show-off: the riding is the thing! The ponies are stubborn, wilful brutes that often need to be physically pushed, or pulled by the tail into position.

The girls and young women are an astonishing sight. Gold teeth glinting, sombreros

20 On the streets, a young performer of the Chinese discipline of qigong *awes and delights passing spectators.* Qigong *literally means "breath skill" but is in fact an exercise for tapping and utilizing dormant powers within the body through breath control and deep concentration. Even brutal acts can be performed on the body without damaging the practitioner. This boy is doing a balancing trick after the ordeal of being bound tightly by wires, which he then breaks by expanding his chest. "My colour is yellow now. I will go from yellow to brown to red to purple to black. When I turn black the wires will burst." He does and they do.*

jammed firmly on their heads, they wear their hair narrowly plaited, African-style. Ultra-violet rays, which they receive from the sun less impeded by cloud than on the plain, have burned their cheeks rosy-blue. Many of them wear silver milk-bowls hanging in rows down the backs of their ornate robes. The bowls indicate the wearer's family wealth, and each one costs months of butter-making from the milk of the patient yak.

A few decades ago these women would have had several husbands — usually brothers — so that babies could still be conceived while most of the menfolk were in the higher plateaux during summer. Nowadays it's one woman, one man.

To an outsider's eye, the girls are mostly plain, with prominent teeth and small noses. But there are stunners there too — giving tantalising sidelong glances with a faint smile, hinting at great curiosity, and readiness to be amused or pleased. One of the girls often bursts into raucous laughter at things that have been said or she thinks were said. The language, alas, stands between us like a fence, for not many of the Tibetans will admit to speaking Chinese.

We while away the afternoon in a smoke-filled tent, sitting on the floor behind a long table loaded with barley meal, yak butter, milk-tea with salt, iron-hard twists of fried bread, big bowls of sugar, sweets brought by the guests, and hideous, cold mutton chops plastered with fat. To drink, alas, there is no *chang* or barley beer today — only a sweet wine from China and some appalling grain spirit. A bowl of yak yoghurt helps relieve the stomach discomfort caused by the altitude of some 10,000 feet.

All this time they have been peeking at our cameras, and at a word from the chief photographer they form into a dense but well-disciplined circle which he shoots piecemeal from the middle. Everyone desperately wants a Polaroid shot, but natural good manners make the people shy to ask. Otherwise get one of the literate ones to scratch his name and pasture area on a piece of paper, stick it on an envelope after developing the films in Peking, and send it off with a prayer that the Chinese censorship won't deem it seditious ... Anyway, there will be more visitors along soon with Polaroids: the Chinese have tumbled to the tremendous tourism value of the Tibetans — who inhabit not only Tibet, but large areas of other provinces as well, especially "China's Switzerland", Qinghai, and Sichuan, which the Chinese call "the kingdom of heaven".

As we drive off, I spot a single, red-robed lama of the Yellow Hat sect, sitting cross-legged all on his own in the grass, gazing towards the foaming shore of Lake Kokonor in the distance — perhaps meditating, as casually as one would read the newspaper. Everything else in the landscape is blue and pale green and white; only the lama's robes make a contrast.

Monasteries are being reopened: just a few of the biggest and most famous ones. At Kumbum, in Qinghai, centre of the Yellow Hat sect — dominant in Lama Buddhism — the faithful come from Japan and Thailand and Sri Lanka, to stick coins with yak butter to an ancient, holy stone under a *bo* tree. Two hundred monks — mostly novices — sit in a semi-circle chanting the wonderful sonorous prayers of Buddhism in deep voices, and grinning over their shoulders at the tourists. Old women prostrate themselves completely on wooden boards guarded by big prayer-wheels. A little girl is peddling yoghurt at the temple gates. Mongols, Khambas and even Chinese Muslims arrive in the charabancs, fingering tawdry goods in the souvenir shops — horses' bits, stirrups, colourful woven cloth, Buddha statues.

The Tibetans have very few personal possessions. The standard ones, for the men, are shoulder-robe, breeches and leather boots, a felt hat, a knife in a chased sheath, sometimes an ancient rifle with forked prongs at the end of the barrel to rest it on an upright stick or branch for better aiming.

The women have more religious objects — personal prayer-wheels and rosaries, stupa-shaped amulets containing prayers or an old photograph of a famous lama, perhaps the Dalai Lama. Their favourite stones are turquoise and coral. With these they will part for a modest sum, but they rarely sell their prayer-wheels. And the Chinese authorities have now banned all trading in antiques with foreigners.

How are the Animals?

The Tibetans were once a serious military power in Central Asia. But in the West people think of the Mongols, and the Turkic peoples called Tartars, as the terrifying horde that reached the gates of Vienna and held Russia in subjugation for a couple of centuries.

So it comes as a surprise to find the Mongols to be some of the most amiable people in Asia, living very close to nature, self-contained and cheerful where they have not been tempted or dragooned into the dismal industrial life of northern China.

China's two and a half million or so Mongols outnumber those of the Soviet-dominated Mongolian People's Republic, farther to the north, by about two to one. In China more of them are settled in mud-brick houses than live in tents (the Mongol word is *ger*; the word *yurt* is Turkic).

The *ger* is one of the snuggest dwellings ever devised by man. Being circular, it has no corners for the steppe winds to snatch at. The former hole in the roof has been replaced by a stovepipe and a glass skylight. Inside, cushions and little cabinets are scattered around, while the residents take their ease on rugs covering the grass.

When visiting Mongols, it is considered good manners to ask how the animals are — for their illness spells economic loss and even disaster for a herding family. Worst of all is the dreaded *dzud* — the late spring frost that freezes over the fresh grass and leaves the animals to starve. Horse, sheep, buffalo, camel, yak, and *hainag* — a cross between a steer and a yak — are the only real wealth of the Mongols, apart from what they may have salted away in a socialist bank at the nearest township, at a very modest rate of interest.

The Mongols have three great loves: riding, wrestling, and drinking mare's milk. The last of these is becoming rarer, since the milk needs long hours of patient stirring to ferment evenly into the wonderful drink called *airag* (*kumiss* is the Turkic word). With the residue, they make a fairly potent alcoholic drink called *argh*. The root of these words is found throughout Asia and the Middle and Near East to mean strong drink — *arak,* for instance. But only the Mongols make it out of milk.

Not only is the milk of various animals a staple of Mongol life, it has medicinal qualities too: the people say that the milk of a white camel will cure tuberculosis. Alas, there seems to have been no lactic cure for syphilis, the plague of the Mongols until recent times. One still hesitates a little when offered a puff of some aged Mongol's pipe.

The rest of the Mongol diet is dreary. They put mutton fat and salt in the tea they brew from iron-hard dark-green bricks sent all the way from southwest China. They also dump some roasted millet in it, and millet is a tasteless enough food even when it is boiled soft. There are lumps of rocky cheese to gnaw at, and the best thing is just a haunch of mutton, boiled and carved in big chunks with an ancestral knife. Nobody goes to the Mongols for their gastronomy — even the famous "Mongolian mutton hotpot" is an invention of the Chinese, designed to disguise the flavour of the mutton, which most Chinese dislike.

They are great narrators and singers — my wife and I once got an accolade in a *ger* for a rendering of *Waltzing Matilda,* whose sheep-stealing theme they could identify with immediately. Old lamas, defrocked long ago but now gradually retrieving their religious identities, preserve folk-cures for illness and keep alive their Tibetan-style Buddhism, which the older generation of Mongols cherish to the point that they revere Tibetans as having a special spiritual quality. They build little cairns of stones and leave offerings on them — a tiny aluminium coin, a scrap of food, an unspent cartridge. And although they love and revere all types of life, they are realists and sportsmen who hunt foxes across the steppes on horseback — or in a jeep if there is one handy.

Justifying their meat-eating habits, a senior lama once told me: "It was always very difficult to be vegetarian in Mongolia."

One of the most touching scenes was when an Outer Mongolian journalist — representative of his country's news agency in China — came upon an ancient Mongolian monk at Wutaishan, a near-unbelievable complex of monasteries and stupas tucked away at the top of a 5,000-foot valley in the wilds of Shanxi Province, still sacred to the Mongols. Shouting over the monk's deafness, the little Mongolian newsman quizzed him in the strange, biting language of their race, which seems to consist mainly of r's and z's. I didn't, of course, know what they were talking about, but the Mongolian exchange of courtesies, across centuries of the race's division and decline, made me feel something special had happened. The exploits of Genghis Khan, Khubilai Khan, Ivan the Terrible (who threw out the Mongols from Russia), Stalin, Mao, Brezhnev and Deng, for a moment seemed small compared with this miracle of a few million kin-linked people flung across four thousand miles of Asia. Mongolians are found as far west as the Volga still today.

The Tibetans live with their heads halfway to the skies, the Mongols are rooted firmly in the grassland. At great gatherings or festivals — to which some may come hundreds of miles — they race their ponies, and their champions wrestle grimly on the hard earth. A nineteenth-century Mongolian general in the service of China once picked up an overbearing British Consul-General and threw him into an ornamental pond.

They have not the Tibetans' tremendous flair for colour and colour combinations, but they love colour nonetheless, and there is no garment more becoming than the belted calf-length robe or *del*, with a pair of plain black knee-length boots showing below. The women, dressed in clothes more enticing than the Tibetan women's long and frankly rather dirty robes, have never practised polyandry, only polygamy. But the sexual tastes of the men — as shown in old paintings — were frankly eclectic in the past, not excluding erotic interest in the animals. Doubtless all this is frowned on today.

Life in Tibet is a battle with nature in which all imaginable spiritual and magic forces are supposed to be invoked. In the places of the Mongols, it is a less eerie and more down-to-earth affair in which superstition and faith certainly play a role, but the less austere living conditions make people more easy-going and materialistic. A television set looks less incongruous in a *ger* than in a Tibetan tent.

Asia Deserta

For two thousand years past, China's soldiers and merchants have repeatedly probed the huge region around the Takla Makan — the desert where "you go in but don't come out," as the name means in rough translation from Turkic.

On its fringes there sprang up Buddhist kingdoms in the period of Europe's Dark Ages, incredibly rich and sophisticated little civilisations which drew on the cultures of India, Persia, and China. Guarded by garrison forts of mud brick, and straddling the Silk Route used by traders going as far west as the Mediterranean, the Buddhist kingdoms such as Turfan and Khotan created rich traditions of dance and wall-paintings, some of the latter

25 These three young women have come from distant areas of Yunnan Province to take part in song and dance competitions. The victors will go to Beijing to perform for the top leaders of the country. The woman in the middle is a Lisu; the other two belong to different branches of the Yi minority.

26 An actor in a moment of reflection between scenes. He is part of a troupe that travels from market town to market town in the north of China. He and his itinerant friends from Shandong Province live by their wits, performing as clowns, acrobats, jesters and comic bumpkins. The government neither supports nor interferes with their way of life, a sign that many forms of hitherto dormant cultural expression may be allowed to flourish again.

being discovered only around the beginning of the twentieth century and carted off to Europe by orientalists and explorers.

The murals — the most famous of which survive at Dunhuang in Gansu Province — did not fare well under the rule of the Turkic tribes of Central Asia when the latter were converted to Islam. Religiously opposed to the painting or drawing of the human form, Muslim fanatics poked out the eyes of all the painted faces at Bezeklik, one of the richest sites. The rest of Bezeklik's murals were bombed to fragments in the Berlin Museum during the Second World War.

The whole of Xinjiang (Sinkiang) — also known as Chinese Eastern Turkestan — was incorporated formally into the Chinese Empire as a province in 1884, though Chinese garrisons had controlled it militarily for over a century before that. Among the notable oasis cities is Turfan, which the Chinese call Tu-lu-pan, lying at the feet of the so-called "Flaming Mountains", the name being derived from their red colour and the flame-like configurations of their slopes.

Turfan is surrounded on all sides by desert, the nearest rivers being in the Tianshan mountains to the northeast. The desert is partly shingle, partly sand, and has an amazing feature: man-made water channels some eighty feet under the surface, connecting up natural wells and guiding the water towards Turfan.

At the very edge of the oasis the miracle occurs. At the point where the cool, sweet water comes bubbling out of the desert slope, the land explodes into greenery, supporting lush grass, fruit trees, vines and melon patches galore.

The grapes and melons are famous throughout China, though the wine made in Turfan is mostly disappointingly sweet.

Apart from fruit, the local people live off a diet of flat bread, rice pilaff with mutton and carrot-shreds, and various spices and dairy products. These are the people known today as Uighurs. Of Turkic stock, they dress unlike the Chinese: the women wear floral-pattern, knee-length cotton skirts or dresses with ugly thick brown lisle stockings, Western-style jackets and embroidered skull-caps. The men have knee-length boots, two-piece suits and skull-caps. They move around on small donkey-carts, carrying produce to market or making purchases of modern consumer goods from the factories of China proper.

There are very few Han (ethnic Chinese) to be seen in Turfan: at most, a soldier from the garrison haggling over the price of vegetables in the bazaar. And what bazaars! Lamb and mutton for shashliks, peppers, carrots, spices, melons, flat bread, tobacco-leaf, wines, skull-caps, seeds, boots, embroidery, trinkets, saddles and bridles, brassware — in short, everything needed for a busy farming community with its ancient roots in the desert and in Islam. The one thing not on sale is the Koran — which, being written in Arabic, can be read only by the mullahs and muezzins anyway. Attempts by the Chinese authorities to suppress the Islamic faith have now been largely abandoned, and the mosques are well attended. The Arabic script — long banned as an affront to the Chinese regime — is back in favour.

The favourite occupation of the Uighurs is dancing, and every man, woman and child can go through the sinuous, graceful arm-and-body movements and steps of the Arab-influenced art-form, accompanied by wailing, Middle Eastern music quite different from that of the Chinese. Every Sunday there are weddings (as Sunday is the day off work), and strangers are welcome in off the street to sit on the married couple's bed-platform and eat pilaff with their hands.

The midday temperatures in summer can exceed 40°C, and people don't trifle with the heat like "mad dogs and Englishmen". Their houses have deep cool cellars, where they take refuge until the sun declines somewhat. The nights can be decidedly chilly.

Near Turfan lies the deepest depression in East Asia where the salty Lake Aidin glistens

28 The Wuyi Mountains of Fujian Province are difficult to reach and still rarely visited by tourists. "Each peak is a single rock, each single rock becomes a peak". The ascent to some of those peaks is dangerous and requires careful footwork on nearly vertical stairs chipped out of the stone face. Some cliffs at Wuyi have caves that were once repositories of sampan-shaped coffins, dating from nearly 4,000 years ago.

malevolently in the bright sunlight. Nothing grows, not a blade of grass, for miles around, and drinking water has to be trucked in. A few hundred benighted workers from Shanghai operate a chemical plant making sodium compounds. The young have no entertainment but the wireless and a concrete ping-pong table. If they venture too far out onto the salt crust at the edge of the lake they may be sucked in and disappear. With an inner shudder, one reboards the bus for Turfan.

The Small People

Nowhere in the world has a greater variety of races and nationalities than Southwest China. Their stock is related to the Tibetans, the Burmese, the Chinese, the Thais, the Khmers, or the Polynesians, or of obscure origin. Their costumes and ornaments are incredibly varied, especially featuring delicately-worked silver. They live off the wooded mountainsides and terrace their village fields independently of the Han Chinese. They speak dozens of languages and dialects and many of them practise various forms of free love.

Scholars are still bewildered by the multiplicity of small nations and tribes in this part of the world. Some have even suggested it may contain the earliest traces of *homo sapiens*. Some of the bronze-work done by southwesterners rivals that of the Hans in technique and perhaps antiquity.

Like most mountain-dwelling people, they are probably refugees from the historical expansion of the stronger, more populous races which surround them. Traditionally the Chinese despised them, but feared their archers and raiders.

Today the southwesterners are supposed to be incorporated into the unitary Chinese state. But they have suffered much bullying at the hands of the Chinese as recently as ten years ago, as is now regretfully admitted in Peking.

Some races — the Naxi and the Yi, for instance — have their own written languages, evolved quite independently and, in the case of Naxi, consisting of quite explicit coloured pictures. The Yi script resembles the runes of the Norsemen and the old, now largely forgotten script of some European gypsies (not that any genetic link is suggested — nearly all scripts begin as pictures.)

Most of the southwesterners — Miao, Wa, Bai, Li, Yao and others — are mountain-dwellers, who practise slash-and-burn cultivation, now discouraged by the Chinese authorities because of its wastefulness. But in coastal Guangxi Province and on the large island of Hainan, they have become more settled and cultivate coconuts and sugarcane, shooting deer and squirrels and birds for food, and for their skins and feathers, and sending some of their young people off to serve in the Chinese armed forces or to attend university.

Most of the southwestern minorities do not follow any organised religion, but the older people especially practise a form of primitive animism, in which spirits are believed to inhabit particular trees, rocks or streams, and need to be appeased with incantations or offerings. Shamanism, a form of Asian witchcraft, is also to be found, but is discouraged by the Chinese authorities.

The biggest of the southwestern ethnic groups are the Zhuang, people loosely related to the Thais, who inhabit large areas of Guangxi Province and are fairly well integrated with the Chinese.

Another group is the Dong minority of Guangxi, Hunan and Guizhou, which numbers approximately one million. They are compulsive builders, making bridges and waterwheels on their river banks, the wheels being moved automatically by the running water. Water-powered stone hammers used to be wielded to pound their rice, to make rice flour.

One of the largest groups are the Miao, closely related to the Hmong of Laos and Vietnam. A warlike race, the men used to carry swords whenever they left their villages, and they are skilled with the crossbow. Their traditional singing is accompanied by clappers and drums, and by wind instruments. The White Miao, a branch of the group, used to have a singular custom: when a man was about to be married, a hammer and chisel were used to knock out two of his teeth "to avert the mischiefs of matrimony."

Another tribe cultivate maypole dancing as a form of courting, and most of the Miaos used to practise free love in a single big hut — a custom which shocked the encroaching missionaries as much as the Chinese communists. Still today, in some places, women may have several lovers before they choose the right one for marriage — a custom repugnant to the Chinese. Though the Miao are mainly settled farmers, some of the wilder groups still practise the mesolithic life-style of hunting-and-gathering in the forests. Like most of the southwesterners, the Miao are great weavers, especially skilled with small handlooms held in the lap of the women weaving.

Another once-warlike group are the Yi, related to the Tibetans, and historically divided into Black Yi and White Yi. They practised an elaborate form of slavery in the past and warred continually with the Chinese. The Black Yi were the main landowners before the communist land reform. The White Yi worked as serfs or freemen under the landlords. The Whites practised skilled trades and could read and write, something the Blacks thought unnecessary (like the early Plantagenet aristocracy in England). Petty warlords used to fight each other, and opium became an important crop in the 1800s.

Many of the southwesterners have no means of written communication except by such primitive methods as notching wood or tying knots in string. The Peking government has attempted to introduce new scripts based on the Roman alphabet for the nearly 1.5 million Yaos, cousins of the Miao, who live in northwestern Guangdong, southern Hunan, Guangxi and Yunnan.

Disease, famine and warfare were reducing the numbers of the southwestern minorities in the first half of this century. The relatively orderly conditions prevailing since the communist armies occupied the southwest, and the improvement of local medical knowledge, have reversed this trend. Small nations have also been exempted from the national birth control programme — but only temporarily. Eventually they, too, will be ordered to have no more than one child per couple, perhaps two or three in the deepest countryside. But the importance ascribed to having big families still persists.

Minority customs and costumes are particularly rich in mountainous Yunnan Province. Furs, embroidery, and silver hoops and filigrees adorn the brilliantly coloured costumes of the women in particular. The richer a girl's family, the more silver finery she will wear on festival days. Coins are used to make buttons and necklaces; some of the older women have tattooed faces. There is an abundance of elaborate hair-styles. Skirts are both short and long.

Picturesque and fascinating as China's small peoples may be, an inner tragedy inhabits any ethnic group that tries to live in a style not much advanced beyond the neolithic. Like aboriginals, Eskimos and New World Indians, the social ecology of such peoples is fragile. A Chinese official said in my hearing in Kunming: "Of course eventually their languages will be forgotten and they will all speak Chinese."

31 The wrathful eyes and twisted mouth of this guardian deity camouflage his goodness and devotion to the Buddha. He stands thirty feet tall and guards the entrance to Hua Ting Si, a Ming Dynasty temple outside Kunming, Yunnan.

The Sea of Faces

Fascinating though the 50-odd million minority peoples are, the vast, pulsing machine called China is run first and foremost by the Han — the ethnic Chinese, having their racial origins in the Yellow River basin.

Growers of grain since before recorded history, the Han have centred their culture on that simple but laborious process. Their early artifacts are dominated by vessels in which to store or cook grain, ornate jugs from which to pour the liquors brewed from grains, ritual vessels from which to offer libations to Heaven.

The dependence on grain led inevitably to the establishment of huge, settled populations guarded against floods by enormous earthworks and tapping the rivers for water to speed their seedlings' growth. Politically they were subject to rulers who taxed them.

Now the peasants are again pursuing private farming, and for the first time ever there are no heavy exactions on their produce, only a modest tithe to help feed the city-dwellers. These millions of soberly clad workers strolling or cycling down the avenues of China's big cities are the providers of hard cash to the government. The profits of their factories are taxed, providing four-fifths of government revenue. The peasants feed them on grain at a low cost specified by the authorities. And they in turn make consumer goods for sale to the peasants.

In between the essential strata of society — the workers, the peasants and the leaders backed by the army — are the so-called cadres or officials and intellectuals who do not work with their hands, but tell others what to do (advice which is often not welcome).

At long last China's cities are beginning to show signs of sprucing up. At the same time, the bugaboos of modern urban life are appearing: Peking, where one used to be able to drive at a fair speed almost anywhere with no more hindrance than traffic lights and a few policemen, is becoming a wheezing, creaking mass of near-stationary traffic, particularly in the rush hours when one is now stuck among buses and trucks, taxis, and even "honey carts" (nightsoil removers).

The mood of the city dwellers, notwithstanding the growing traffic problem, is more buoyant than it was a decade ago. The girls and young women are actually making themselves pretty in the summer with diaphanous dresses and wide sun-hats, and the young men sport often incongruously-inscribed T-shirts.

A huge transformation in Chinese urban life since the time of Mao Tse-tung is the flowering of entertainment for the masses — not just inspirational political songs and dances, but family dramas in the cinema and theatre, modern light music over the radio, foreign music and films, and greater variety of television programmes.

The scope for learning new sports and competing both nationally and internationally has also been widened. Whereas previously Chinese ping-pong players had dominated the sporting scene, footballers, ice-hockey players and even wind-surfers are now encouraged to bring their skills up to international standards. Women volley-ball players are national heroines and have rocked the entire sporting world with their prowess.

But above all it is the new availability of consumer goods that has fired the people's vision of a more comfortable and elegant life for themselves and their children. The most popular float in the 1 October National Day parade bore a huge cardboard fridge with tiny human figures around its base, admiring it. The same longing is felt for washing machines.

The Chinese are not yet exactly in a consumer revolution; outside Peking, Shanghai and Canton they experience frequent shortages of both basic and ancillary goods, while many of the new products are faulty and break down and cannot be easily repaired. This will change, of course, but it all takes time.

33 *The tropical lushness of Hainan's countryside holds promise for future agricultural exploitation. Pepper, rubber, cocoa, coffee, tea, sisal, hardwoods and rice are already products of economic significance. The island also has a rich ethnic mix. Li people came to Hainan 2,000 years ago, the first human inhabitants. Since then waves of Miao, Zhuang and Han have arrived and a small Muslim minority (2,500 people) grew from the crew of an Arab ship that ran aground on a Hainan beach.*

35 *A Buddhist monk holds a sheaf of newly printed scriptures. He is a member of an anachronistic institution, the Dege scriptural printing house. Dege, located along the vital Chengdu-Lhasa highway, has the largest collection of Buddhist woodblock plates in the world, more than 200,000 pieces. The rarity of the collection, the printing methods employed and the quality of reproduction bring orders for scriptures from Buddhist communities throughout the world.*

An astonishing combination of patience, self-indulgence, resignation and ambition defines the mood of the Han people today. They know exactly what they want in the short term — more goods and services — but their longer vision has been obscured by too much political in-fighting at the top, too many twists and turns in the leadership's policies.

The one billion are set on enjoying the good things of life, and are mostly prepared to wait a while longer to see their world prosper and become generous. The leaders know this, but they also know there is a limit to the people's patience. Some things have to take priority. Pollution, despoliation of forests, growth of raw and ugly new towns — these are the costs of progress. China's land is so vast, and so much of it quite unspoilt, that she may still avoid some of the worst pitfalls of industrialisation which other countries have fallen into before her. Nature has given her a sporting chance. Let us hope she does not throw it away.

David Bonavia

The Northwest

36 *Each year the Langhsan Festival brings together Tibetans from seven counties within the Tibetan Autonomous Prefecture of Gansu Province. Many types of competition are held, including yak races, lassoing, wrestling, tug-of-war and horse-racing. The jockeys are young boys.*

38, 39 *A camel caravan heads out into the barren wastes beyond the Great Wall. It leaves behind the two lone sentinel towers of Jia Yu Pass in Gansu Province, the traditional terminus of civilization. Classical writings abound with terrible tales of China's deserts, and the sorrows that follow from any journey beyond the safe bounds of Han culture. Merchants lured by profits of trade carved out the Silk Road, but thousands lost their lives, even in recent times. The Swedish explorer Sven Hedin gives a gruesome account of six days without water in the Takla Makan, a western extension of the Gobi Desert. Camels' urine and vinegar, which the desperate men resorted to, provided no relief. Hedin finally reached a river but most of his expedition died under the blistering sun.*

40, 41 *"Roads: good for ten years, bad for ten thousand". As one goes farther west, the roads become rougher and rougher or entirely non-existent. Runaway water from heavy rains and melting snow has made this highway nearly impassable. Transport is a perpetual problem throughout much of China and here, in western Sichuan, delays have serious consequences, for these trucks carry vital supplies of fuel, machine parts, grain and medicine.*

42, 43 *In the highlands of Gansu
Province a joyous ritual takes
place. The site is a sacred
mountain eight miles from the
famous Buddhist monastery of
Labrang. "Planting of the
Arrows" both propitiates and
invokes protection from the
mountain spirits. Long, colourful
staves, one for each family, are
planted in a symbolic circle within
a corral. Only males do the actual
embedding, and the act protects
the whole family for a year. The
entire arrangement is sanctified by
smoke from fires of yak butter
and* tsamba, *the Tibetan staple of
parched barley.*

*As much noise and revelry as
possible enhance the celebration.
Conch horns and wild gunfire, in
this case from an automatic rifle,
echo through the valleys.*

44 *The Uighurs of Xinjiang are Turkic speaking peoples, linguistically related to the Kazaks, Uzbeks and Kirgiz. They number 5.5 million, and their facial features show antecedents from farther West.*

45 *Despite common borders, the enormous size of China's western administrative regions guarantees the isolation of certain minority groups. There is virtually no way a Uighur of Xinjiang could ever meet this young woman. She is of the Tu minority who live exclusively in Qinghai, number only 160,000 and speak a Mongolian tongue of the Altaic language family. Traditionally, Tu girls had to marry by fifteen or lose the chance of a socially sanctioned marriage.*

46 In southwestern Gansu
Province performers take a rest
backstage between episodes of
historical dramas. These dramas
enact stories of valour, religious
super-heroes and titanic struggles.
This performance is one part of a
larger festival. The "woman" on
the right is in fact a man in a
female role. In feudal China,
prevailing notions of propriety
and ideals about women's virtue
required a strict segregation of the
sexes, with the women usually
confined behind closed doors.
(The name for a wife, "nei ren"
— inside, or kept, woman —
neatly epitomised this view on the
role of women.) In the theatre
this meant that men and women
were forbidden to play on the
stage together, so young men had
to be trained to impersonate
females. They underwent special
training, involving study of body
movement, gestures and falsetto
singing.

47 *Arable land on the Qinghai-Tibetan Plateau is scarce and high altitude severely limits the types of crops. This man carries his harvest of barley, the staple food of the area. Parched barley flour mixed with tea forms the main meal, day or night, and fermented barley beer is the local intoxicant. Barley, the most ancient of all cultivated grains, is marvellously versatile, able to be grown at altitudes up to 15,000 feet. Barley straw is soft and can be used for bedding or as a bulk roughage feed.*

48 In Kashgar, most remote of all large Chinese towns, a Muslim cemetery bakes under the harsh sun. This oasis city of the Xinjiang Uighur Autonomous Region is strategically located less than two hundred miles from the borders of four nations: the Soviet Union, Afghanistan, Pakistan and India. Over the millennia Xinjiang has been a melting pot of settlers and invaders: Aryans, Scyths, Yuechi, the Huns and Wusun, Turks, Mongols and Hans. In the more recent past it was the arena of intrigue and contest among Britain, China and Russia to dominate that part of Central Asia in their struggle for ascendancy in the East. Today twelve minority nationalities live in Xinjiang.

49 *Qinghai Lake, called Koko Nor, the Blue Lake, by early Tanguts who inhabited the surrounding area, is an enormous inward-draining salt sea, the largest of its kind in China. Bird Island, a protected conservation area, and nearby waters are home to a multitude of birds. More than 200 species have been identified so far. The birds shown here are cormorants.*

50, 51 *The Karaxahar flows in silvery loops through the high grass plateau of central Xinjiang, nearly 10,000 feet above sea level. Mongols live here, not the predominant Uighurs of Chinese Turkestan.*

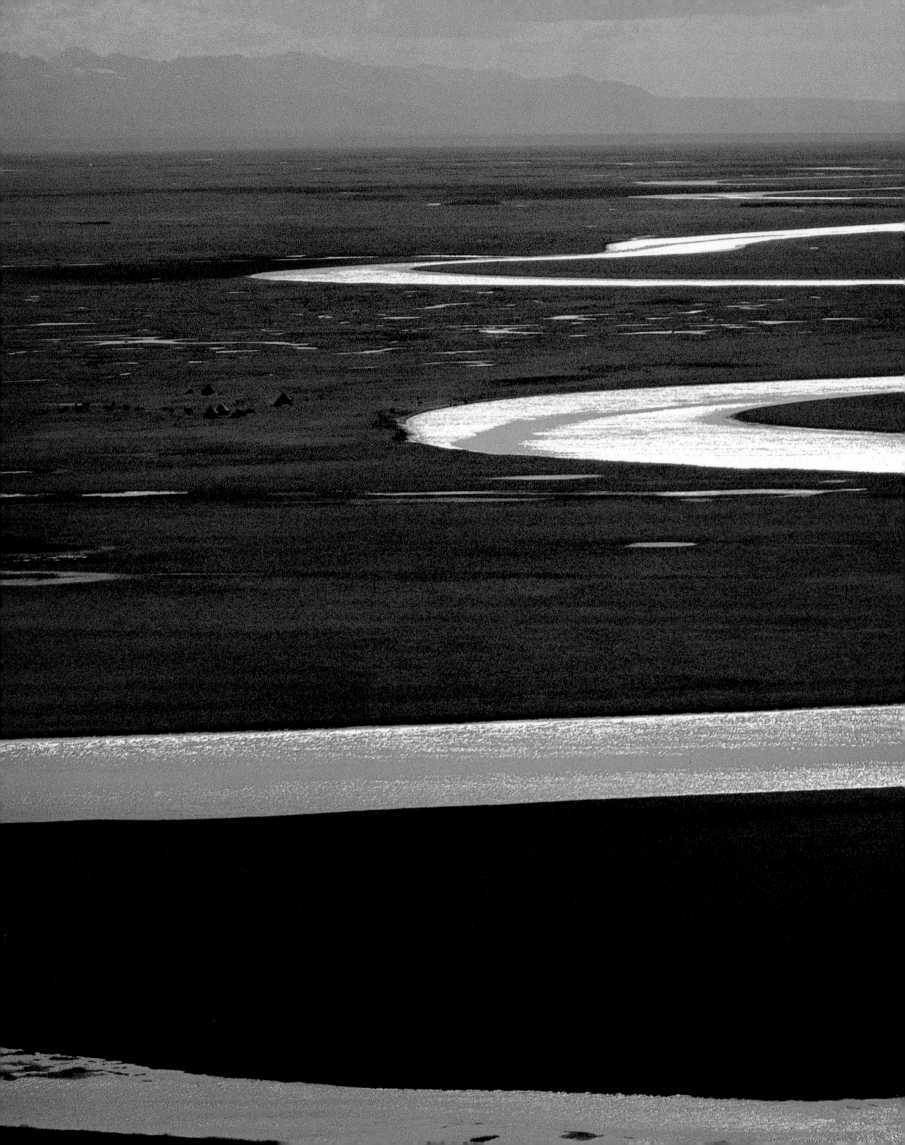

52 *These yellow-capped, maroon-robed lamas have gathered for a theological debate at the monastery of Labrang in Gansu Province. Labrang has been a major centre of Buddhist learning since 1709 and its authority extended to 47 other monasteries in the region.*

53 *Members of the Muslim population of Lanzhou, capital of Gansu Province, come out to pray near the Yellow River. This service marks the Islamic New Year. The Muslims are known as Hui in China, and their faith distinguishes them from the majority Han. They came to western China during the Tang Dynasty (618-907), flourished and finally gained ascendancy over Buddhism in the fourteenth century with the fall of the Mongol Empire. The majority Han Chinese have never assimilated or fully subdued the Hui.*

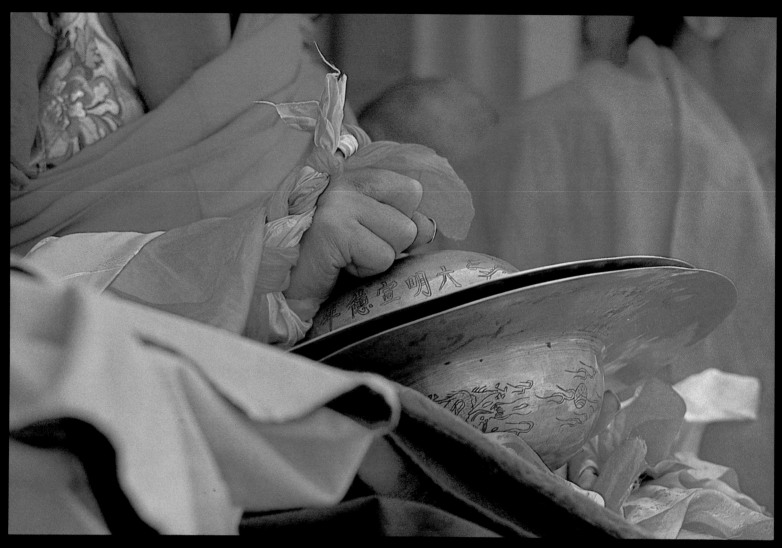

54 Clashing cymbals and pounding drums animate masked dancers who portray ghosts, deer, and mythic beasts. The lamasary of Ta'er Si, better known as Kumbum, was founded in 1560 and is the largest in Qinghai. Religious persecution during the Cultural Revolution took grotesque forms, affecting all faiths and millions of people. Only in very recent years has there been a revival of religious life and lay Buddhist response, especially among Tibetans, has been profound.

55 Buddhism came to China by way of the Silk Road, leaving in its wake sites of unsurpassed religious art. Maijishan in southern Gansu is a major Buddhist cave center, developed between the fifth and twelfth centuries. A single oddly-shaped hill contains over 190 separate caves with approximately 1,000 pieces of sculpture, which are some of the most interesting examples of China's artistic heritage. Some images on the soft rock have been eroded by a thousand years' exposure to the elements, but most have survived. Hellenic features are clearly visible in many of Maijishan's statues and are bold historical reminders of influences that reached China through Afghanistan, India and Central Asia.

56 *Deep in Central Asia, the great dunes of the Takla Makan Desert are reminders of China's geographical variety and grandeur.*

57 *Under a rising moon former nomads have gathered on the Songke grasslands of southern Gansu for an annual festival. Beautifully embroidered tents have been used for generations and once again provide shelter to these Tibetans. They have brought along their prized possessions, including a television set. A high-ranking lama in the next tent will share power from his portable generator.*

58, 59 *A Kazak wedding takes place on the grasslands of Qinghai. Although nuptials are now conducted as civil ceremonies, traditional custom still guides the proceedings. After displaying the marriage certificates, various preparations are made. Horses and camels, indispensable creatures of nomadic life, are loaded with the dowry: food and articles of daily use. The bride is then slung over a horse like a sack of barley and carried off to be delivered to the husband's family.*

The Southwest

60 *A Yi farmer enjoys his pipe in the rugged Yunnan-Sichuan border area. The Yi are the fourth largest minority group in China, numbering nearly five million. They are scattered broadly through the mountains of Yunnan, Sichuan, Guizhou and Guangxi.*

62, 63 *Originally a goat path, this road is hacked out of the rock high above the Min River in Sichuan Province. No tractors, bulldozers, or power tools whatsoever are used. The Qiang minority people who live in this region are building the road to open an isolated, backward area to transport and commerce, a clear but awful example of the emphasis placed on communication and economic development.*

64 *In the late spring of 1935 the Dadu River of Sichuan proved to be the most difficult obstacle of the Red Army's Long March. Had the Communists been thwarted by the Dadu, they almost certainly would have been defeated by Nationalist forces. The almost unbelievably courageous capture of the Luding Bridge, a span of thirteen swinging cables, allowed the Red Army to continue northward towards its eventual revolutionary base at Yanan. Even today it is not easy to cross the river.*

65 The waterfall of Huangguoshu is the largest in China, falling fully 220 feet. The oranges of Guizhou give it its name, "yellow fruit tree".

66 *The mountains of south-western China are cleaved by great rivers and inhabited by many distinct minority peoples. These Qiang women have just crossed the Heishui River on a wooden platform suspended by cables, and hauled across by hand.*

67 *The silver amulet of this Khamba horseman contains a miniature Buddha image, worn for good luck and as an act of devotion. Kham is the huge area of southeastern Tibet whose people are both nomads and settled agriculturalists.*

68 *A gentleman of Sichuan carries*
all of life's necessities with him.

69 *The habitat of the yak lies between 14,000 and 20,000 feet above sea level; these long-haired oxen languish at lower altitudes. On the Qinghai-Tibetan Plateau yak dung is the only source of fuel. Yaks also provide transport, milk for butter and cheese, hair for felt and ropes and hides for warmth. The tail also makes a good fly whisk.*

70 Guizhou Province, one of the poorest regions of China, has been given the unkind epithet of a place where "there are no three days of sun, no three li of flat land, and the people lack even three taels of silver". This woman lives by growing chilis.

71 Tobacco was introduced to China from the New World, as were red chilis, corn, peanuts and potatoes. Smoking is a ubiquitous habit in China, though done almost exclusively by men. Tobacco can be quite cheap if purchased in the street markets as dried leaves or shredded shag. The cigarette industry is tightly regulated by the government. The Guizhou farmer (right) likes the option of smoking either a pipe or cigarettes.

72, 73 Black Miao of eastern Guizhou are celebrating a wedding. Most women wear predominantly black costumes, a few of which have lovely red sleeves. This indicates that the woman is over seventy years old, an elder of the community. (She will in due course be buried in those same clothes.) Men will join in later, but only after these women have beaten the drum all over — on the leather heads, on the wooden sides and on the rims.

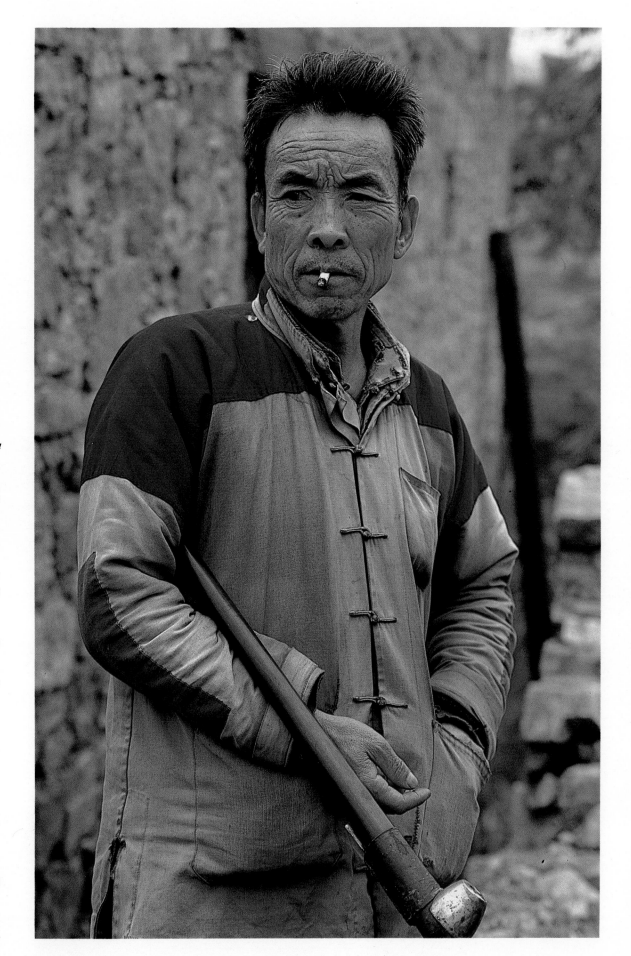

74 Every village has its teahouse where the elderly can sit and chat all day long. These men are joking about the village's first son to go to college: "a dung beetle wearing glasses".

75 State-run shops such as this one still account for the great majority of retail outlets in China. However, small cooperatives and family enterprises have proliferated over the past several years, responding to the needs of China's enormous population. Restaurants, bicycle repair shops, tailors, cobblers and street vendors are some of the more conspicuous businesses that have sprung up.

76 Southeastern Yunnan, near the Vietnamese border, is populated by the Zhuang and Miao minorities. This woman of Yanshan is a White Miao. Her high bee-hive headdress is part of the daily attire she wears for digging and weeding in the fields.

77 A Sani girl adjusts an earring just before opening her vegetable stall for market day. The Sani, a branch of the larger Yi minority group, live around the famed Stone Forest of Yunnan. They are a strong, capable people who have produced many warriors and political leaders.

78 *A branch of the Yi minority lived under a hierarchical slave society that lasted until the late 1950s. Travellers entered the Great Cool Mountains of Sichuan at their own peril, risking enslavement or death. Today slavery has ended and life under the Chinese government improves steadily for the Yi people. Happily they have not entirely relinquished ethnic individuality in personal decoration, as this girl — wearing the deeply-dyed costume of old and all her lovely ornaments — displays to charming effect.*

79 *A herding family travels through the marsh meadows north of Kangding in Sichuan Province. Yaks, sheep and goats make up their flock and provide most of life's necessities. Kangding is the traditional gateway into Tibet from China.*

80, 81 One of the world's most remarkable geographical phenomena is found in the region where eastern Tibet and Yunnan Province come together.

Amidst 20,000-foot peaks, three mighty rivers flow parallel to one another, north to south, before diverging and following their separate ways to the sea. At one point only fifty miles separate the Yangzi, Mekong and Salween Rivers, although their mouths are thousands of miles apart.

Here a tiny hamlet perches on steep banks of the upper Salween. With its source in the desolate Tibetan Plateau, the river, known as Nu Jiang in Chinese, tumbles and flows 1,500 miles to the Gulf of Martaban. The Salween flows through a continuous gorge to within seventy miles of the sea and is thus practically useless for navigation.

82, 83 Tibetan cavaliers show off
their finery after a display of
expert horsemanship.

84, 85 *The Jinuo, only recognized as a separate minority group in 1978, number approximately 10,000 and live within the wild mountains of southern Yunnan. They come down from the highlands on rare occasions for major markets and festivals. Here they have been invited by the regional government to join other minorities in celebration of the Water Splashing Festival.*

Slash-and-burn agriculture is slowly supplanting their traditions of hunting and gathering. Even so, a totemic deer always accompanies Jinuo rituals, as does a huge drum whose rhythms induce a trance-like state during dances.

86 An orchestra of Naxi men play Yuan Dynasty (1271-1368) music at a friend's birthday party. Northwestern Yunnan, home of the 240,000 Naxi, did not become part of the Chinese empire until Kublai Khan came south with his conquering armies. The music played today is a legacy of that time.

87 A cold dawn breaks over Lake Dian as these fishermen head for their fishing grounds. Sadly, proximity to the industry of Yunnan's capital, Kunming, has meant increasingly polluted water. Soon the entire lake will be unfit for fishing — a consequence that highlights one of the dilemmas of China's modernization drive.

The greatest Chinese maritime explorer, Zheng He of the Ming Dynasty (1368-1644), grew up on the edge of Lake Dian and, as a child, must have paddled about in a similar skiff. Later he was to visit the East Indies, Ceylon, Arabia and the east coast of Africa as leader of a huge sailing fleet.

88, 89 Living quarters upstairs share this huge building with a night market below, Tibet.

The North

90 Legend holds that a great cypress tree was planted by the mythical Yellow Emperor, original ancestor and first sovereign of the Han people. He brought civilization to the human race, introducing pottery, metal, weaponry and the wheel. This Chinese cypress stands at Huanglin in Shaanxi, site of the tomb of the Yellow Emperor.

92, 93 Zijincheng, the Purple Forbidden City of Beijing, was the imperial palace for most of the Ming (1368-1644) and all of the Qing (1644-1911) Dynasties. Although the Forbidden City is now open to the public, it will never yield up all the secrets of its past. The inner intrigues and treacherous plots of thousands of court eunuchs will remain forever unknown.

94, 95 A sea of soldiers at a People's Liberation Army parade. The PLA, largest standing army in the world with six million regulars, is trying to modernize its weaponry and tactics after decades of reliance on guerrilla warfare.

94

96 Mongol wrestlers go at each other in an age-old martial sport, in which the object is to unbalance the opponent and throw him to the ground. The sport has recently enjoyed a resurgence in popularity and is a part of all public gatherings on the grasslands.

97 Outside the walls of Beijing's Forbidden City, soldiers show off the new uniforms of the People's Liberation Army. Insignia and indications of rank are symbolic of recent broad changes within the army.

98 *Kite-flying is serious recreation in China. Each year there is an international competition where hundreds of varieties of butterfly, goldfish, crane, phoenix and centipede kites fill the sky. Some individual kites need a hundred people to launch, but this enthusiastic pensioner prefers to fly his alone.*

99 *This special side-car for the transport of a beloved child has many features: glass windows and curtains, a paper lantern for decoration, a ready bottle and a hinged roof for easy access. "Precious as jewels, the children give us hope."*

100, 101 The Hulanbeier region of Inner Mongolia is home to nomadic herdsmen. Warm dry winds have blown for several months and now, at the end of summer, the grass is parched and stunted. Even so it provides adequate pasture, because each family grazes its livestock on a section of grassland that is separated by huge distances from the nearest neighbour.

*102 This Mongolian woman
guides her Bactrian camel with a
steady hand. Although slower
than the Arabian camel, the two-
humped Bactrian can maintain its
pace over a longer period. It is
able to carry a load of 500
pounds twenty-five miles a day
for three days without water. The
camel is found throughout
Central Asia and is used widely as
a beast of burden.*

103 *A photographic studio uses historical props to whimsical effect. The Chinese character on the breastplate,* chuang, *means "charger".*

104 *Representatives from all fifty-five of China's recognized minority groups are brought together annually for meetings and festivities by the central government, ostensibly to promote unity among the diverse populations. This gathering is in Inner Mongolia, homeland of the 2.7 million Mongols within the borders of China.*

105 *A Mongol tightrope-walker proceeds with his act despite winds and the absence of a safety net.*

The Northeast

106 *A modern-day "lamplighter" changes bulbs at a railway station in the industrial Northeast.*

108 *Tram lines in the snow, Harbin. Heilongjiang and its two provincial neighbors to the south, Jilin and Liaoning, form a region that western geographers call Manchuria. In Chinese,* dongbei, *the Northeast, refers specifically to these three provinces. Since 1900 they have grown remarkably in population, agriculture and manufacturing, with heavy industry the hallmark of the area today. China's oil industry is concentrated around the vast oil fields of Daqing in Heilongjiang.*

109 Steam power still drives
many of China's trains today.
The first permanent railway in
China was built in 1881 but lack
of capital deterred the Chinese
from expanding their own rail
network. Imperialist powers filled
this gap and most railroads were
built during the first fifty years of
this century. Only under the
Communists has a truly nation-
wide rail system been established.

110, 111 Harbin largely owes its origin to the Chinese Eastern Railway, begun by the Russian government in 1877. Prior to that time it was a small wheat-market town, poor and isolated. Harbin is China's most northern provincial capital and clearly shows this early Russian influence in its architecture. Known as the "Moscow of the Orient", tens of thousands of Russians lived here, especially after the 1917 October Revolution.

112 Children play and others go
about their business outside a
Russian-style house in
Heilongjiang. The sign on the
door indicates the house has
become a private enterprise for
processing woollen sweaters.

113 The crane is a symbol of longevity in China and Japan - some of them live to eighty years or more - and is celebrated as the bird-chariot of sages who wander freely through the heavens. The Zhalong Nature Reserve near Qiqihar was established for the protection of more than 300 types of birds, including this rare Grus japonensis.

*114, 115 Vast untouched plains
form the border between western
Heilongjiang and Inner Mongolia.
Unlike areas to the south where
land utilization is extremely
developed, here in the north less
than half of the arable land has
been put to use. Even so the
Northeast is a surplus food
producer and has fine potential
for becoming an agricultural
dynamo.*

116 *The frozen Songhua River*
separates Harbin, Heilongjiang's
capital, from Sun Isle. These
commuters are following the same
route serviced by a ferry in
summer. In spring, dynamite is
used to speed the melting process
of nature and free hundreds of
boats trapped in the ice.

117 *The winters of Northeast China are bitter, with temperatures below freezing for up to six months of the year. The growing season lasts only about 160 days, and some areas have permafrost in the subsoil. Cultivation is limited primarily to corn, kaoliang, millet, soy beans, winter wheat and sugar beets.*

The Southeast

118 Water buffaloes continue to provide an essential source of power throughout southern China. These lumbering beasts are indispensable in many places for ploughing, turning mills and preparing new rice fields. At livestock markets a buffalo sells for over US$500.

120 "The Land of Fish and Rice" south of the Yangzi River is considered the richest area in China, with its fertile soil and abundance of water. Centuries ago, land here was brought under cultivation by irrigation schemes, while trading was facilitated by a fine system of inter-connecting canals. Here a boatman guides his string of small barges along one of these narrow canals.

121 At the edge of the Grand Canal, a young boy looks out on a ribbon of water and a way of life that go back more than 2,000 years. Built with simple tools - hoe, shovel and basket - and immense manpower, the Grand Canal is a marvel of engineering and hydraulic construction. It stretches 1,500 miles from Beijing to Hangzhou in Zhejiang Province and ranks with the Great Wall and the Pyramids of Egypt as one of mankind's great achievements.

122, 123 A little fishing village on Lamma Island shows that Hong Kong is not all high-rise buildings and electronics shops. Many areas of Hong Kong are only accessible by boat and give a very different picture from the one that all but a few visitors take away with them.

124 Kaiyuan Monastery of Quanzhou, Fujian was built in the seventh century. In the grounds are two identical pagodas of exquisite masonry, each octagonal and five storeys high.

125 Ropes, brushes, whisks, hats, hampers, chicken baskets, chopsticks and many more items are available at this seaside shop in Fujian. The province is almost entirely mountainous and life in the interior has traditionally been poverty-stricken and precarious. Consequently most Fujianese have sought a living from the sea as fishermen and traders and many went abroad to start a new life. The Chinese communities throughout Southeast Asia largely originated in Fujian.

126, 127 Boatmen pole their bamboo rafts down the Moyang Jiang in southern Guangdong. This area around the town of Yangchun is a watery richness of hot springs, lakes, waterfalls and rivers.

128 *The clear water of Nine-Bend Stream winds its way through the entire Wuyi Mountain region of Fujian, between pine forests and canyons of sheer granite.*

129 *The Grand Hotel, Taibei, Taiwan.*

130 Within the walls of a seventh century mosque, Muslims prepare a water buffalo for slaughter. The sacrficial festival of Qurban Bayram marks the end of the Mecca pilgrimage and is celebrated by Muslims everywhere. Here, the Hui community of Canton will feast for three days in and around the Huaisheng Mosque. Slowly the government is permitting a limited number of Muslims to visit Mecca each year. In 1984 more than one thousand made the pilgrimage.

131 A cyclist transports his geese and chickens to market in spite of their protestations. The Chaozhou people of eastern Guangdong, with a cuisine famous throughout the world, consider crisp-skinned roast goose among the very finest of their dishes.

132 The coconut palm, symbol of the tropics, is found all round Hainan Island. These palms flourish best close to the sea and, when cultivated in plantations, provide an important source of income in the form of copra. Marco Polo was among the first Europeans to describe coconuts.

133 In the tiny territory of Macao, a lone priest walks the corridors of an empty seminary. The Portuguese came here more than four hundred years ago and established a virtual monopoly on trade between China and Japan. Merchant and missionary activities helped build a powerful, prosperous colony but the decline of Portugal's empire and the rise of Hong Kong have steadily eclipsed Macao's role in the China coast trade. Nevertheless the city, clinging to the Guangdong coast, continues to survive despite its somewhat anomalous status of a Chinese territory under Portuguese administration.

134, 135 Sundown at Huangshan, the Yellow Mountain, Anhui Province.

136

136 The Wind and Rain Bridge, so named because of the shelter it affords from the elements, was constructed by the Dong minority in Guangxi. The Dong are renowned for their mechanical and architectural skill. This bridge, built in 1916, contains no nails, only joined timbers and tile work.

137 Each year Dong women celebrate dual festivals, known as the Spring Club and Autumn Club, to guarantee a good harvest and a safe year. Joyous and beautifully adorned with silver, the women also use these celebrations as a time to seek a lover.

138, 139 Sunrise on the Li River, Guangxi.

140, 141 A fishing fleet heads to sea off the east coast of Hainan Island. In the shallow waters of the surrounding continental shelf a massive exploration is on for oil. The South China Sea, from Hainan to the Pearl River, is already being drilled for significant deposits of the black gold that will help finance China's modernization drive.

142 *Bountiful in flora, fauna and minerals and blessed with an easy tropical climate, Hainan's lack of development still constitutes something of a mystery. Throughout history Hainan was considered a frontier region, but today a wave of changes is slowly and steadily moving across the island. This trend is true for all of China as roads are pushed through, airports built, harbours modernized and communications extended to the most remote regions. A broad cultural assimilation is taking place and much of the unique, diverse and special quality of China will disappear forever.*